Ted, The 'Welsh Goat' Hero

Memories of a Proud Welshman and WWII Veteran

by Ted Owens

Published in 2019 by Pembroke & Monkton Local History Society
www.pembrokeandmonktonhistory.org.uk

PEMBROKE & MONKTON LOCAL HISTORY SOCIETY

Supporting Pembroke Museum

Foreword

SINCE I finally opened up about my wartime encounters, many people have suggested that I commit my memories to paper. This summer, in my ninety fourth year, I decided to do just that. I hope that I serve to inform and amuse.

My philosophy has always been to live each day to the full. What I have to say is what I have experienced and not fiction or a second-hand account.

No account of my life would be complete without acknowledging the help, care and support of the following individuals:

I owe a great debt to Debbie and Graham Beacham my 'unofficial' daughter and son. Their care of me has been exemplary.

Journalist Greg Lewis was the first person to take me to France so I could participate in the commemorative events held there.

David O'Toole is a good and supportive friend for whom nothing is too much trouble.

Peter Kraus, ex-mayor of Pembroke Dock and member of the West Wales Maritime Heritage Society, is a close friend.

Pete Bounds, a local professional photographer and master surfer, has assisted with some expert photographs for my project, while Keith Johnson worked painstakingly on the layout of the book; his diligent research for additional photographs revealed some surprises.

Special thanks to Shobha Edgell, who thought that my venture was a good idea.

Thanks also to John Evans and Stuart Berry (Heritage Centre Manager) of the Pembroke Dock Sunderland Trust, and to Linda Asman, Chair of Pembroke and Monkton Local History Society for their help in getting this memoir published.

Ted Owens,
Pembroke Dock, November 2018

Contents

Cover photograph courtesy of the Imperial War Museum (A 26276).
Front cover photo of Ted courtesy of Martin Cavaney.
Back cover portrait courtesy of Peter Bounds Photography.

Surf and Turf – Growing Up in Pembroke Dock

MY NAME is George Edward Owens and I was born on 12th August, 1924, in Neyland, Pembrokeshire. Twelve months after my birth, I moved with my family to Pembroke Street, Pembroke Dock where they kept a public house, The Olive Bar. My maternal grandfather owned the house and was very strict. He was boss. This meant that he and my father never got on.

My grandfather was a severe disciplinarian. I could never open up and talk to him. He would, however, take me out with a gun. I had to walk three paces behind him, never at his side.

He taught me all about the countryside using my senses of sight, hearing and smell. He taught me to smell a badger and a fox which I can still do today (over eighty years later). He taught me what grows in the hedge, what was good to eat and what was bad for you. He was extremely authoritarian, teaching me to catch different animals and birds for food.

When I was about eleven years old I nearly drowned at Hobb's Point. This resulted in me suffering from an acute case of aquaphobia. For three and a half years, I would not venture anywhere near water. I was quite content, however, to go down to the shore, simply to watch the boys swimming. Over the years I got closer and closer to the riparian fun but the nearest I got was 150 yards from the water.

One day I was present as a spectator of the mermen at play, when two local boys were pushed over the jetty. It was a macabre trick as neither boy could swim and one was clasping the other and refusing let go, in sheer terror. I was told that the two boys were drowning. No responsible adult was present and, without thinking, I kicked off my shoes and dived in.

I grabbed one boy by his long, blond hair. I managed to pull both boys out. One was called John Lloyd and the other, who was referred to as deaf and dumb in those days, was called John Evans.

Childhood home: The Olive Bar in Pembroke Street is on the extreme right of this early postcard view.

I was cured of my fear of water which would pay dividends later when I was on active service in France. I met John Lloyd's wife a few months ago (2018). Mrs Lloyd said that John was her late husband. She thanked me for enabling her and John to experience thirty seven years of happy married life.

During the Depression of the 1930s, food was extremely scarce. The food sources I tapped ranged from sheep to 'foul fishing'. I shall share an innovative method of catching fish which my grandfather taught me. I would seek out brackish tidal ponds such as those at Carew or Pembroke Mill Pond. Here I would sprinkle the surface with bread crumbs and grain to attract fish such as grey mullet.

When I thought I had a good sized shoal I would put two table spoonfuls of carbide into screw-top glass flagon which had been used for beer. The carbide would have been collected from old lamps. Then I would tie a lead weight to the bottom of the flagon.

After that I would wee into the flagon causing the urine and carbide to combine. The top was then firmly screwed on and, using a piece of string which had been tied around it, the flagon was carefully lowered into the water so as not to frighten the fish.

The warmth of the urine would hasten a chemical reaction in the flagon. Between five and ten minutes later the flagon would explode. Dead fish would float to the surface as their bladders, which kept them under the water, would have been burst by the explosion. Since I would be wearing a swimming costume under my clothes, I could undress speedily and dive under water about six feet deep to harvest my catch. Whilst the method was questionable it worked and enabled this youngster to assist his family in keeping food on the table.

Another cruel fishing technique was to take a branch out of the hedgerow, about seven to eight feet long, and attach eight to ten treble hooks to it. This vicious tackle comprised three hooks connected to each other. A two ounce weight would be fastened to one end of the branch, which was then lowered into the water. As a shoal of fish approached, I would draw the branch across the water and 'foul hook' the fish – brutal but effective. It all made good eating.

An additional supply of food emanated from the slaughterhouse at Bufferland. Assuaging hunger combated squeamishness. My grandfather had tutored me well.

The slaughtermen were glad I was keen to dirty my hands and learn the trade when not attending school. My education was served better here than in the formality of a school room.

The slaughtermen schooled me in the arts of swift dispatch of sheep and pigs. Cattle were a different matter, being so large; I was not involved in their slaughter. It was important to us that the animals did not suffer.

A swift slitting of the jugular vein and a sheep was no more. Pigs were slit from belly to throat. I knew most of the vital spots for a humane kill. I learned the art of butchery and could joint carcasses ready for the butcher. Little did I know how this tutoring would benefit me during the impending war years.

My grandfather had taught me a highly questionable but efficient method of catching ducks. I would attach a crust or kernel of corn to a hook and cast it to the ducks bobbing on the water, often at the Mill Pond in Pembroke. The ducks would ingest the hook and line. I would then reel them in and stretch their necks to finish them off quickly.

A similar method was used for pheasants as they wandered about in the woods. I would simply cast the baited line onto the woodland floor close to the birds. Once a pheasant had eaten the tasty morsel on the end of the line, I would draw it in, stretch its neck and put the trophy in my bag.

At Barafundle Bay, before fishing I would take a battery torch and inspect the ground at the base of tree trunks. Here I would recognize the colour and consistency of crow and pheasant droppings. Having marked off where pheasant droppings were located I would go off to fish. On my return I would shine the torch up into the trees where pheasants were roosting.

Fishing for pheasants. Cartoon by Jim Titley.

The pheasants would stick their necks out to look at the light. They do not fly at night so they remained stationary.

Having constructed a loop at the end of my fishing rod, I would pass the rod up, hook the loop around the pheasant's neck and yank it down. It was as simple as that. I would stretch the pheasant's neck to kill it before adding it to my bag of fish.

THE war came along (WWII) when I was fifteen years old. I tried to join the Home Guard just to get a gun. I was too young, but I thought I would not be beaten and would join the fire brigade instead. I was made a messenger boy straight away.

Something was holding me back, however, as I had left school with a guilty secret. I was left-handed and even at school I was persecuted. People thought it was just laziness, but today it is known that it is something connected to the brain. My grandfather would give me a whack with his stick if I used my left hand and it was the same at school.

Ted joins the fire service.

If I did not write with my right hand, teachers would stick me at the back of the class and put a dunce's cap on me. Naturally, I kicked up, rebelling against this unwarranted cruelty and humiliation, refusing to learn. I left school illiterate, unable to read or write.

Having joined the fire brigade, I was very ashamed of my lack of literacy. I asked the telephone operators to help me read and write. Three of them took up the challenge and I thanked them for it. Their names were Miss Haggar, who was the sister of Len Hagger the cinema owner in Pembroke, Peggy Gibby and Miss Sabido. Within six months I could read and write. The girls would help me during our night shifts if there were no emergency calls.

Being a garrison town, I would go where the men were billeted and fetch them down if we had drunk soldiers and sailors who wanted to chat the girls up. Very rarely did it happen, but it did from time to time.

During quiet times, when no sirens sounded or anything like that warning of attack, all that my grandfather taught me was gainfully employed. I used to cycle down to Stack Rocks to catch rabbits.

All I used were a two inch wooden chisel and one with a slightly longer handle. On my way down to Stack Rocks I would stop in the hedgerow and cut a bramble about two feet long.

I would then go to the cliff tops and frighten the rabbits. If they went into the main berry I would not bother because it was extremely deep. Also there were play holes which the rabbits enjoyed digging, sometimes for nests. I would stick my bramble in the hole and twist it gently.

If I encountered resistance I knew there were rabbits in there. If I pulled the bramble out and it was all covered in fur I knew it was from a nest and would leave it alone. I would measure on my stick how far into the burrows the rabbits were.

I would use the chisel to open up the entrance so I could get my rabbit. There were many kicked and bruised fingers involved in this particular activity. A profitable excursion could yield as many as eight to twelve rabbits at a time.

Also, I used to collect every birds' egg available, especially seagull eggs, which were strong and fishy tasting. These were less conservation-aware times and food was not plentiful. I would come home with a basketful of eggs and not only those from seagulls. It could be pheasant, swan and anything else which was edible.

I would take a V stick and prod the swan. She would stand up and hiss. You dare not get too close as a swan could give you one hell of a whack. If there was an egg I would take my sock off, put it over the V stick and make a little pocket. I would poke the swan again, which would stand up. I would push the sock under the egg and gather it up that way. It was a small thing but it provided food for the family. People would not think of doing that today.

Pinching eggs from a swan's nest could be dangerous! Cartoons by Jim Titley.

Anything that was fit to be eaten I would bring home, from fish to elderberries. I used to keep all the people in three streets around me in food. I would share with them; food was never for money.

We used to exchange things such as a cabbage for a rabbit. We always swopped, never taking cash.

Understanding the bartering economy helped me a lot when I joined the services.

Firemen's hoses snake up towards the oil tanks fire at Llanreath. Picture courtesy of the Pembroke Dock Sunderland Trust.

W E HAD the bombing of the oil tanks in Pembroke Dock. Today, one can see photographs depicting the conflagration on display at the Pembroke Dock Heritage Museum in the dockyard. It was the biggest fire in the country, bar the Great Fire of London. That was the nearest to it.

The inferno raged for eighteen days. There were hundreds of firemen there. I was there for three days and nights, running messages. There were no canteens or anything like that in those days. We had no organization.

I used to go to the gardens of houses at Llanreath. Here I would collect as many apples and bottles of water as I could, from around the houses where the residents had been evacuated. I used to feed the men with the apples and water, which they accepted with gratitude.

The Home Guard were meant to be guarding the village, but they never saw me. I would sneak past them when I could. I knew all the short cuts.

On the late afternoon of the second day of the fire, I went up to a fire chief standing on his engine and offered him an apple and a drink of water which he found very refreshing.

I looked back across the fields, towards the coast. There was a plane flying back and forth over Merrion Camp. I said to the officer, "that is a German plane." He responded, "are you sure son?"

I replied, "yes sir, that is a Dornier D17." He looked at

The Dornier bomber approaching. Cartoon by Jim Titley.

me and I continued, "it is nicknamed 'The Flying Pencil'."

That must have a tweaked a note with him. He rang the alarm bell. In response, the bell in the next fire engine in the distance was rung and so on. All the firemen, who numbered in hundreds, came running out into the fields, away from the ferocious blaze which they were currently tackling.

The plane came in very low and I could actually see the front-gunner. He never fired into the men, only into the raging firestorm. He dropped four bombs. Why he did not shoot the firemen, I will never know. It is a mystery.

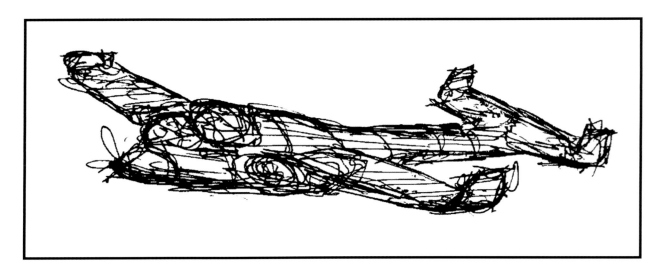

'The Flying Pencil'.... Above: Dornier bomber cartoon by Jim Titley.
Below: Dornier D17Z by kind permission of the Battle of Britain Historical Society.

Aerial photos showing the burnt-out remains of several of the Llanreath oil tanks, while others still belch out smoke.

Pictures by kind assistance of Derek Elliott, Central Register of Aerial Photography for Wales, Welsh Government.

The aftermath of the oil tanks fire can be seen in this aerial photograph from 1946. Also visible are several dozen redundant warships beached on the mud of West Pennar to await their fate, many of them having been obtained from America under the lease-lend scheme.

Picture by kind assistance of Derek Elliott, Central Register of Aerial Photography for Wales, Welsh Government.

The flames were so intense that nothing organic survived. Of the five brave firemen who died in the conflagration, nothing but metal, such as belt buckles and buttons, survived. My shrewd assessment of the looming threat was never formally recognised, however.

When I was sent home from the oil tank fire, I walked into my house and my mother was very angry as I had not told her where I was and what I was doing. Someone had told her I was one of those burned at the oil tanks – no wonder she was angry and relieved.

Bomb damage at the bottom of Gwyther Street. Picture from the Roy Hordley Collection..

She said, "get into the back kitchen and get those oily clothes off you!" I was stinking. Mum tried to wash the oil off my neck and ears and up my arms. My grandfather walked in and my Mum said to him, "Dad, I cannot wash this oil off Ted." He turned round and in his gruff voice bawled, "use paraffin woman!"

No-one came near me for weeks as I stank of paraffin, apart from which it made my skin peel.

THEN we had three nights of bombing in Pembroke Dock. For its size, the town took a beating. I saw many terrible things as I looked for messages and things like that, after bombs were dropped. I saw things that no man should see. There are too many to write down. Some were funny and some were very bad. I shall leave it at that, I think.

The Germans dropped sea mines on the town and I saw one coming down. I innocently remarked, "oh look, it is a parachute."

It went off and there was a huge explosion on the other side of the market. It flattened Market Street, Cumby Terrace, Princes Street, Pembroke Street and half the market hall.

The blast hit me like someone giving me a big punch. I went flying backwards through the door of the fire station. My colleagues said that I was propelled past them like a rocket.

I woke up with the girls at the fire station washing my face which was covered in dust and debris. I was actually knocked out. I was a bit shaken but no harm was done to me.

During the bombing of Pembroke Dock, a number of unaccountable things occurred after the explosions. The blast would produce some peculiar results. For example, one house and shop in Bush Street was completely gutted.

The owners were both killed but they had a young lady lodging with them; her husband was in the Air Force. The owners had insisted that the lady shelter under the stairs – the safest place in the house. The blast travelled through the passageway, knocking the child out of her arms.

The baby, who was about six months old, was discovered in what was left of the kitchen. Luckily both mother and child survived.

Ted outside a building near Hobb's Point that he remembers stabling mules for the Army during WWII . Photograph by Pete Bounds.

On the road to Hobb's Point stood a two-storey, brick, army building. It contained guns and limber – two-wheeled box carriages containing ammunition. When horses pulled gun carriages it was placed between them and the gun.

Men were stationed in this building. A mine was dropped on the beach just below it, on the foreshore. The building was completely sliced off, just above the tops of the ground floor windows, for nearly 100 yards. The upper storey was never reinstated – what remained simply had a new roof put on it.

The building is still in use today; I was photographed in front of it in November 2018 (right). There is also a photograph (opposite) of me in front of a building further down the road which was used for stabling mules during the war. This shows what the damaged building originally looked like when it still had two storeys.

A T CRITERION Corner, again on the way to Hobb's Point, there were three hotels. All three were completely flattened. This included The Pier Hotel, where a large number of people were at a party when it was hit by a bomb.

The only survivor was a young lady who worked in one of the hotels. Tragically, she lost an eye. The land has not been rebuilt upon, and remains grassland. It is not known how many people were killed there.

When I arrived all the rescuers were busy searching for survivors. I sought out the man operating the water pump and asked if there were any messages for the station. He said that there were none. Everything was under control.

This long, low building on the right of the road to Hobb's Point lost its second storey to a wartime bomb. Photograph by Pete Bounds.

17

He did ask me to hang around however, as he could hear voices emanating from somewhere. I walked a little way from the engine because of the noise.

I heard sounds coming off the foreshore, which is opposite where the police station is today. I climbed over the wall and onto the beach when I heard the sound in front of me again. I pinpointed the utterances to a grey parrot, still in its cage.

The cage and its avian inhabitant had formerly been hanging in the foyer of the Criterion Hotel. The dimensions of the cage had been about two feet by three feet. It had now been compressed to the size of a football with the unfortunate, crouching bird within. The blast had projected it seventy to eighty yards from the hotel and onto the beach.

I took the cage back to the pump man, informing him that the occupant was the source of the 'voices' which he had heard. He cut two of the wires on the cage so that the poor old thing could stick her head out. I took the survivor

The Pier Hotel was completely destroyed by a parachute mine.

back to the station and we made a cage for her, out of a tea chest.

Our guest enjoyed fire brigade hospitality for about six months. Finally she was returned to her owner, Mrs Gill, the former owner of the Criterion Hotel. Mrs Gill's only complaint was that her formerly refined pet now swore. Obviously the parrot had used her time with us profitably, grasping the opportunity to expand her vocabulary.

On another occasion after a bomb dropped, I saw one airman dead at the side of the road without a mark on him.

His companion, who lay not five yards away, was completely smashed to bits. Both had been killed by the effect of the blast.

One incident was most unusual. A bomb dropped on the Barrack Hill. This dislodged a telegraph pole which now protruded from the ground like a javelin.

The Dolphin Hotel in Pembroke Street was a large private house during this time. A large bomb was dropped behind the hotel in the lane, which blew all the windows at the back into the house itself. It also blew all the front windows and their frames clean out and onto the road.

There was a little sweet shop next door. A group of us went to see if the occupants were all right. They were very badly shaken up. A young girl of sixteen could not find her

The displaced parrot. Cartoon by Jim Titley.

shoes or the young son of the house. I carried the young lady on my back to the fire station because of all the broken glass on the ground. Fortunately the boy was found and carried back by a fireman. Thankfully their parents had survived.

I continued with my duties. When I was 16 years old, I was sent to train as a dispatch rider for the fire service.

I went to the school where these American bikes had been delivered. They were the 'Indian' model; ex-police bikes sporting 1000cc engines. What a treat for a sixteen year old country youngster in wartime Pembrokeshire!

I used to pick up messages from all the fire stations in Pembrokeshire. This would take me about four hours. I would then deliver them to HQ in Carmarthen.

Life progressed as I carried out my duties with the fire brigade. Little did I know what the war held in store for me as I approached adulthood.

19

Training Tactics

WHEN I was eighteen years old, I was called up to the services. I put down for the Navy and my brother put down for the Air Force. They stuck him in the Navy and I went to the Royal Marines in Lympstone, Devon.

It was a Royal Marine training camp. I did all my training during my three months there and passed with flying colours. I was then transferred to North Wales, to train on landing craft.

Whilst I was there, a message came through, to select all the men with the highest grades in everything. No explanation was given. We were told to pack our kit. Our group was herded onto a train.

Eventually we arrived in Scotland. We had a shock to discover that our destination was to be the Commando Basic Training Centre (CBTC). The Centre, based at Achnacarry Castle, represented the pinnacle of military training. It was highly regarded by the Allies and detested by the Germans.

We were expected to find our own way – in double quick time – to Achnacarry Castle which was about ten miles away.   There were arrows on the road marking the route. We were given a deadline we had to meet in reaching it. I managed to get there within the allotted time by keeping up a brisk jog, carrying all my gear. Those who failed this initial test were discharged in disgrace. Once there, we had to 'double' (trot) everywhere from the lavatory to the cook-house.

We were an international bunch. Recruits hailed not only from the UK, but France, the Netherlands, Norway, Czechoslovakia, Poland, Belgium and even free Germans, often Jewish who had escaped the despotic exercise of power in their homeland. Here I was, a Welsh Taffy from Pembroke Dock ready to shoulder the burden of harsh and severe training.

The parade ground at Achnacarry Commando training base. Image courtesy of The Commando Veterans Association.

Ted as a newy-fledged Royal Marine Commando.

The discipline and expectation was intense. There were no safety measures or wires to help anyone on exercise. If you did not do it correctly, you were hurt. Today it is a requirement to have a safety harness, clips etc. In those days, if you lost your balance or grip and got injured, it was your hard luck.

Some recruits died during training. Live ammunition was used, as this was not a game, but preparation for the theatre of war. Those who failed to reach the required standard were RTU'd, meaning that they were returned to their units.

The emphasis was on physical training. I had a good foundation in many of the topics to be covered on the syllabus. Survival skills I had learned from my grandfather.

In Pembrokeshire, I had spent time travelling over rough terrain at night searching for food. This was to assist me with silent execution skills and night manoeuvres. I was not trekking for rabbits, fish and pheasants now, but would be seeking the enemy. The struggle for food would become a battle for freedom.

Some of my fellow trainees, who were townies, would faint at the sight of blood. Having worked in an abattoir, hunted and fished from boyhood, I was case-hardened to the realities of nature. I could use a gun to shoot for food, so weapon handling was not a novelty.

Commandos cross a river on a 'toggle bridge' under simulated artillery fire at the Commando training depot at Achnacarry in January 1943. Image courtesy of the Imperial War Museum (H 26620).

Riding and maintaining the Indian motor bike as a fire service messenger boy, meant that I had an understanding of how engines worked. This was to benefit me when learning about vehicle operation.

My bold and impromptu rescue of the two boys at Hobb's Point and subsequent fishing trips had rendered me fearless of water. I could boast that I had 'sea legs'. I had relied on my head for heights when collecting birds' eggs and catching rabbits on the cliffs of Stackpole. These boyhood experiences gave me a heads up with amphibious and cliff assaults.

Boyish scraps with mates was a very basic grounding in hand to hand combat. Unfortunately, I had no background in demolition, but I was a quick learner.

THE sergeant styled me 'Taffy the Welsh goat'. Perhaps he likened me to the mascot of the Royal Welch Fusiliers. Hardy, lively and frisky described this Capra pretty well.

Unusually for a goat, I was left panting and breathless on brisk uphill runs. My caprine attributes deserted me on such terrain. One could be expected to reach the summit of Ben Nevis, eighteen miles away, during a day's training.

However, if 22 Unit ever had to run on level ground, the sergeant knew I would leave the others standing. I was six feet tall, lithe and willowy. There was no catching me then. Perhaps I was more of a cheetah than a goat, but the sergeant would not consider naming me after such a graceful animal. Taffy the cheetah does not have the same ring about it. We

were there to be moulded into fighting men, not sleek conceited creatures. Flattery was not part of that process.

I passed all my training with top marks. I was presented with my highly-prized green beret by Lord Lovat, the top man who organized the Commandos and was in the camp at the time. His family's tartan colours included the shade Lovat Green, hence the 'green beret'. Today he is commemorated by a monument, in France. It was a great honour to receive it, and to this day I am proud of that green beret.

About ten years ago I was privileged to visit the statute of Brigadier Lord Lovat at Ouistreham looking inward from Sword Beach in France. In the past, French people had kissed me on both cheeks as a greeting, when I attended military functions in their country. It then became the custom to salute with an arm laid across the chest.

On this occasion I laid a cross at the foot of the monument and gave a conventional salute. A young lady aged between 30 and 35 approached and hugged me, then planted a kiss on both my cheeks.

Greg Lewis, a news editor, had accompanied me on this trip and stood behind me. I was very flattered at this welcoming gesture from the young lady. Turning to Greg I said, "this is my first French kiss on this trip as they normally salute now". The poor lady turned as red as a beetroot. Wagging her finger at me she protested that I had the words wrong.

I responded, "no, you kissed me on each cheek, that is a French kiss." My fan objected vehemently crying,"no!"

I was a very innocent eighty four-year-old.

Ted receiving a hero's welcome on a return visit to Achnacarry after an absence of 70 years.

Into Action

AS A fully-fledged Commando, I was transferred to 41 Commando Unit. We were moved around a lot, from town to town but we were entitled to civilian billets.

After I had been there a while, we were loaded onto a train with all the windows painted black, so it was impossible to see outside. The doors were locked. We had to tolerate this for two days and nights. No one knew where we were. These clandestine precautions were taken in case of spies.

We finally reached our destination, which we did not know at the time was Littlehampton. Waiting for us were cattle waggons commandeered from local farmers. This elegant form of transportation was to convey us to the camps.

We were most indignant. All our equipment and lorries had already been taken to the camp. The assistance of the farmers saved on transport costs. To demonstrate our annoyance we stamped our boots, bleating and mooing for all we were worth. If we were to be treated like cattle and sheep, then we may as well have sounded like them. As we moo'd and baa'd, the sergeant major stood at the side of the road shaking his fist at us shouting, "I'll give you baa, you 'naughty' boys." He may in fact have used more expressive language but the memory dims with time!

This was a foreshadowing of what was to follow. We were placed in a camp surrounded by barbed wire. It was grim to say the least. There were Americans on one side of the wire and Canadians on the other. The Americans had the best of food.

I said to one of the Americans, "they are starving us here!" He took my billy-can and returned with a whole chicken and a large spoonful of ice cream by the side of it. That went down well with me and two mates.

We did not have chicken on the menu when I was in the services. It was wartime, prior to mass food production, and chicken was a luxury meat.

We were never told where we were going. However, once we were issued with French money it was clear that we were being deployed to France. We were moved out and onto landing craft. We remained at Littlehampton for 24 hours. Landing was meant to be June 5th 1944, but was altered to June 6th because of the weather.

The weather was stormy but the landing craft were not built for such conditions. It finished up with seventy per cent of the men being seasick. I was not, because I was used to boats (or so I thought).

An order then came over the Tannoy that we were to eat some food, as it was not known when we were going to get our next lot. I delved into my kit bag and recovered a tin of ox-tail soup.

These cans were self heating. They had a little fuse down the centre of the tin which you lit. You had to be careful, as careless lighting could cause the tin to explode. I gulped it down.

Within half an hour I was on deck with the rest of them, heaving over the side, being sick. The combination of a listing boat, fear and adrenalin probably compounded the nausea. I can confidently say that I have never eaten ox-tail soup since.

R M Commandos landing at Sword Beach on D-Day.

Troops on Queen beach, Sword area, sheltering behind troop carriers, June 6, 1944. Image courtesy of Imperial War Museum (B 5093).

When it was time to go onto the beach the Tannoy message was, "take your helmets off, throw them over the side and wear your green beret with pride". I think that was a crazy order.

When we went down the ramp, the noise was terrific. I cannot begin to describe it. War films produced after the war, for entertainment and education, cannot convey the traumatic mêlée awaiting us. The sound comprised tanks, guns, engines revving and ourselves screaming as we went ashore.

We had flail tanks fitted with chains in front of us, exploring for mines. We followed them up the beach.

Another Tannoy announcement ordered us to concentrate on a big hotel on the sea front which the Germans had fortified into a big bunker. There was a lot of machine gun and rifle fire emanating from the hotel.

The Germans were playing 'heck' with us. One of the tanks on my left had been knocked out. I ran over to the tank, laid my rifle across the back end and looked through my sights. I could see Germans moving about inside the hotel, approximately 150 yards away. I fired five or six rounds, I cannot remember exactly.

A shell came over; I do not know if it was a mortar or the shell from a gun which landed on top of the tank. When it exploded, all the shrapnel came down on top of me. I had – and still now have – fourteen pieces lodged in my left shoulder and the scars to prove it.

When the metal hit me I went down on my face but did not become unconscious. I was however, absolutely paralysed. I could not move. How long I lay there, I have not a clue. I then heard a voice coming up from behind me saying, "this poor blighter has had it."

The soldiers turned me over and mercifully my eyes moved. One said to the other, "he's alive!" The men checked me over and patched me up the best they could. They left me there, I do not know for how long, but it was a long time.

The stretcher bearers picked me up and carried me down to a landing craft. I was taken out to sea and hoisted onto a hospital ship. While I was on the ship I was given a new injection called 'twilight sleep'.

Fortunately, I knew nothing further until I woke up in a Cardiff hospital, three days later. I was then moved from there to the Miners' Hospital in Caerphilly.

The medics opened up my arm and shoulder. The wound was kept open in case of infection and dressed with an inch wide bandage soaked in penicillin. Penicillin was also a new discovery at that time. I was incredibly thankful, as my shoulder, scapula and chest were penetrated by fragmenting shrapnel.

When a shell bursts, the metal is white hot. When it touches anything cooler it breaks up again. That is the reason why so many pieces of metal shattered, piercing and lodging in my body.

To this day, fourteen pieces of shrapnel remain in my left shoulder, two in my back and one in my chest. I remained in hospital for two and a half months.

ANOTHER unseen, permanent injury, was to my left ear drum. I had awful ringing in my ear for weeks after the explosion. I now understand that this could have been a symptom of the damage. I fear that the vibration of the blast caused a ruptured ear drum.

I never complained about my hearing loss to the doctors. The blast-induced deafness would become a permanent memento of D-Day. I would just turn my head to hear as a strategy for coping over the years.

Earlier diagnosis and issue of hearing aids would have improved my life considerably. People did not make a fuss in those days.

I suppose I was simply glad to be alive, knowing and seeing that others had not been so lucky.

Tasty Toes and Other Tales!

AFTER I was discharged from hospital I had five days' leave. I then went back to re-join my unit but I was excused all webbing equipment which would have rubbed on my not inconsiderable wounds.

All I carried was my rifle and a side pack. It caused quite a bit of trouble because officers stopped me and asked why I did not salute them! I had to show them my special pass. It was a right pain in the butt (if not my shoulder).

I re-joined my unit in France at Pont L'Eveque. A big battle had been fought there and the Germans had retreated.

You may have seen the caricature of the French fireman drunk on a street corner. I can assure you that it was indeed a reality as I witnessed such an inebriated spectacle for myself. A Frenchman complete with large, silver helmet struggled to wheel his bicycle along the road. He was too drunk to risk riding it.

On spotting me he effusively bellowed out, 'welcome Tommies!' Perhaps 'Taffy' would have been more apt.

He offered me a drink from the bottle of brandy which he wielded unsteadily. I politely refused. I had never liked the smell of spirits even when I lived at The Olive Bar in Pembroke Dock. I found the smell sickly and offensive. I had never tasted spirits in my life. I did enjoy a beer though.

Sensing my reluctance might be caused by fear of poisoning, the drunken fire fighter swung the bottle to his lips. He took a deep draught of his precious liquid. He then offered me the bottle. It was July, I was hot and thirsty so I took a swig. It was immature Calvados. Consequently it was about 99% proof. It was like swallowing hot coals.

I was speechless for a few minutes. I cannot remember the taste of this spectacular libation, but it was bloody hot. The flavour of freedom was too much for me.

We marched all the way through France. Some places I cannot remember. Some had no names.

The beautiful town of Pont L'Eveque in Normandy suffered massive wartime damage. Photo: I.W.M.

At the liberation of Dunkirk we had surrounded quite a few Germans. Our mission was to keep them contained at Dunkirk. We remained there for three weeks without facilities for washing.

When we finally came out of the line we were supposed to be picked up by the transport lorries. Unfortunately we were informed that, contrary to expectation, the lorries had not arrived. Captain Sturges, the officer in charge, told us to eat something and then rest in a barn across the way.

After the meal of mostly tinned products – tasty bully beef from Argentina, similar to corned beef but not the same as products available today and soup (but not oxtail!) – a group of us ventured towards the barn.

We reached the barn exhausted and dirty. We were relieved to remove our boots, socks and clothes and lie on the straw. Completely drained of strength after all that we had endured, we all fell into a deep sleep.

Morning saw the welcome arrival of the lorries. We were being driven to a big, old farmyard. Waiting for us was a mobile shower unit. En route, one of the boys complained that his feet were sore.

Coincidentally, all six of us were suffering the same malady. On arrival at the farmyard one of our group sought out the medical officer (MO), complaining of his morbidly tender feet. The MO immediately became agitated and summoned someone to obtain a receptacle from the farm.

A child's tin bath was produced and filled with hot water and salt. We all had to place our feet in it. After we had dried our feet, an orderly appeared, armed with a bottle of iodine, which was poured directly onto our feet. I had not jumped so high in a long time. We were all missing our toe nails.

I asked the MO how this had occurred. He explained that our toe nails had been gnawed off by rats during the night. The cunning rats avoided our fingernails as fingers contain more nerve endings and we would have been aware of this diabolical night feed. In war-besieged France, food was scarce and the rats were lacking calcium. Hence the feeding frenzy on our toe nails.

Dead horses left out for a week or more, would succumb to a similar fate and have their hooves completely consumed by rats for the same reason. After this unpleasant interlude, there was no sign of any poisoning so we were passed as medically fit and set off again.

WE FOUGHT all the way to the coastline of Belgium. We were always on the coastline. We had lots of small skirmishes in different places. I travelled to De Haan on the Belgian coast near to Zeebrugge. One of our ships had been sunk by a bomb or a torpedo; I do not know which.

I was informed that approximately five hundred RAF personnel had been killed by the blast or drowned in the sea at Knokke. Volunteers were requested to carry the bodies onto the beach. This went on for a week.

After the second day a report was received that someone was stealing from the dead bodies. We then had the job, in twos, of guarding our dead comrades.

We were paired off and my mate and I had the last two hours in the morning. The order was to shoot anyone who was spotted on the beach.

A person had been seen in the early hours, actually going up to some of the bodies and interfering with them. He was shot for his pains. We went down to the beach with a stretcher to collect the body. It was discovered that he was in civilian clothes. There was a bit of a stink because of that.

It turned out that he was a German deserter. His girlfriend came down onto the beach, breaking her heart. She told us that her lover had absconded because of her and hated what the Germans were doing. He had to get money to survive.

She was marched off with the local police and I heard no more of this poignant incident.

THE Germans started firing V2 bombs. These were retaliatory weapons. The precursor was the V1 on a gyro which did not fly as high a V2, which was supersonic. The Germans fired these from thirty miles away at North Beveland in Holland. They travelled quite low and were within firing range of a rifle.

We would take pot shots at them. A direct hit would unbalance these atrocious weapons. This would cause them to crash as they were on an automatic gyro. Orders to cease shooting were issued when one decimated a whole village as a result of our sabotage. We were only to shoot by the sea so that the bombs would land there, away from human habitation.

Our journey continued to Antwerp where I was stationed. A service club, The Union Jack Club, had been set up close to a large cinema to benefit the troops with rest and relaxation. One night a bomb fell on the cinema which was the next but one building to the club. Luckily for me I was down below in the cellar area.

The cinema was razed to the ground. Quite a few people were killed. On the now exposed wall about three storeys up on the left hand side was an alcove. Contained within it was a man actually hanging on. His escape from death was miraculous. He was rescued by the fire brigade. The cinema looked as if it had been sliced away with a knife leaving the buildings on either side standing.

One of the local ladies who socialised with us at the club, invited a few of us home. She selected three of us – me, an army corporal from the Royal Artillery and a soldier from 55 Highland Division. It was kind of her to treat us to hospitality in those uncertain times.

We were her guests for three nights. It was an experience in civility and comfort. The property she lived in was a large chateau with servants. The lady despised the Germans who had occupied her home for a time. That went against the grain for her. I do not know her identity but she was obviously a person of influence, high on the social spectrum.

We returned to Pont L'Eveque. The whole front line was held up by a very large mushroom-shaped bunker rather like a pill box. It took command of the whole of the front. The Canadians, 41 Commando and The Highland Division were held up as the Germans held the commanding view.

Someone called up a Polish tank company. They had a gun attached, which when fired, made one hell of a hole and completely buried the bunker.

We could hear the men trapped inside screaming and shouting. My best friend who was a corporal, a very quiet gentle person, was with me. He approached the bunker and made a hole in the gun ports. He rummaged in his pouch and removed a 36 hand grenade and a 38 hand grenade which contains phosphorus. This will burn anything it touches. He lobbed these into the hole, finishing off the enemy in a particularly horrible fashion.

I was disgusted and voiced my disapproval in Anglo Saxon terms. In plain English I asked if there was any need for such cruel and deliberate action. Nothing was said at the time.

When we returned to the rest area, I brought the subject up. Again I asked if it had been necessary to deploy a phosphorus grenade, killing men who were already trapped.

My friend started poking me in the chest. No one else would have done that to me at that time. I could take care of myself and others knew it. He knocked me backwards; he was so sharp with his gesture.

In his temper he bellowed at me: "Taffy, you have just come back from Blighty. You don't know what the hell is going on. Until you find out, keep your f****** mouth shut."

I was stunned and did not react. When we had time to spare I asked some of my comrades why my friend had become so bitter. He was a changed man altogether.

I was informed that he had the misfortune to discover 14 dead Commandos in an apple orchard in Pont L'Eveque. Their hands had been tied behind their backs and they had all been shot in the back of the head.

This violent episode was the result of an infamous order issued by Hitler dated 18th October 1942 – The Hitler Befehl. This chilling edict contained the following passages, sealing the fate of Commandos including the unfortunate men at Pont L'Eveque.

From some time now our enemies are using methods in the prosecution of war which are outside the agreements of the Geneva Convention. Especially brutal and vicious are the members of the so called Commandos which have been recruited, as has been ascertained to a certain extent, even from released criminals in enemy countries.

Captured orders show they have not only been instructed to tie up prisoners, but also to kill them should they become a burden to them. At last orders have been found in which the killing of prisoners is demanded. Germany will in future use the same methods against these sabotage groups of the British i.e. that they will be ruthlessly exterminated wherever German troops may find them.

I therefore order that from now on all enemy troops which are met by German troops while on so called Commando raids, even if they are soldiers in uniform, to be destroyed to the last man, either in battle or while fleeing.

It does not matter whether they are landed by ship, plane or parachute. Even if they want to surrender no pardon is to be given in principle.

Such an edict would only be permissible in a theatre of war, if the commander, his troops <u>and the enemy</u> are aware of it. The document was top secret and concluded:

I shall have all commanders and officers who do not comply with this order court-marshalled. *

Hitler feared the Commandos' elite fighting skills. His revenge was truly terrible. Those wearing the green beret and carrying the dagger could expect no mercy.

For my friend, the poison lay with those young Commandos lying in the orchard at Pont L'Eveque. As a consequence of what he had witnessed, my friend would aim to shoot German soldiers trying to surrender. The officers had a hell of a job trying to control him. He had developed into a liability, prone to react unpredictably.

The genie was well and truly out of the bottle for this essentially peaceful and kind man. He had become homicidal in respect of the enemy. He only remained with us for a couple of weeks after this incident.

He completely lost the plot. That is what war does to some people. Eventually he was sent home. I do not know how things turned out for him and if he survived the war.

WE WERE billeted at another place in Holland, on a farm. A young Dutch lad on the farm was very friendly. I asked in pidgin English if there were any fish in the river. He replied that indeed there were plenty of fish swimming in the river.

* Source: operationmusketoon.com/capture-https://execution/ hitlers-commando-order. Courtesy of Gavin Worrell.

It was the River Maas (Meuse) which flows through France, Belgium and the Netherlands. I returned to our waggon and took out four hand grenades. I lobbed them into the river.

The resulting explosion caused many fish to float to the surface. My not so subtle take on my grandfather's tuition was an improvement on urine and carbide.

The lad wrestled off his pullover in excitement, filling it with fish. With delight, he went running home to his mother, to show her this piscine bounty. Within half an hour the fish were gutted, cleaned and cooked. What a feast for those hungry times. Talk about feeding the five thousand with my grandfather's help!

We finished up at Zeebruge. A few boys got blown up by booby traps. The Germans were very fond of planting them. One nasty one was called a shoe mine which was like a small, square cigar box nine inches by five inches, something like that. They were hideous little things which would maim you by blowing your feet off.

To search for them, we would gently poke our bayonets into the ground. We would then dig them out cautiously, open the lid and remove the fuse. That was the only metal which they contained. Everything else in these horrors was made of wood.

I captured a German motorbike on the Belgian border near Bruge. It had a Spandau machine gun attached to it. The rider and passenger had been killed but the bike was in perfect working order. I yanked the machine gun off and threw it in the hedge.

Ted wasn't the only one to 'liberate' a German NSU motor-bike and sidecar – these GIs had the same idea!

The bike was an NSU which had a reverse gear. That feature was uncommon for a motorbike built at that time. This was quite a step up from the USA 'Indian' motorbike of my fire service messenger days. I was delighted to run it, without mishap, for two months.

My friends rode in the sidecar. It eased the tension of war conditions and we had great fun. We were stationed at Zeebruge and it was great to be mobile. It was almost a taste of freedom.

One day, a captain from Cardiff asked to borrow it in order to buy some booze for a party. I was very reluctant, but he was a captain and a fellow Taff so I had no option but to agree.

Off he belted down the road towards a Bailey bridge which the army had constructed from steel. Unfortunately a civilian had chosen this exact moment to take advantage of the new route across the river, now available to him. The captain was in a dilemma. Did he hit the civilian or the bridge?

Much to the relief of the civilian (and presumably his family) the captain hit the bridge fair and square, coming to an abrupt halt. The sidecar was ripped off, rendering the bike useless. His riposte to me was, "sorry Taff, I smashed your bike and broke my thumb!"

He must have hit the bridge with tremendous force as the NSU bikes were solid and robust. Still, the bridge remained standing and the civilian survived.

The British army could be proud of its construction skills. I did mourn the passing of the bike though.

AN UNCONVENTIONAL thing happened at a farm in Zeebrugge, where a farmer, asked me for a bar of soap. I presumed that he was trying to maintain basic standards of hygiene despite the terrible privations people were suffering.

I obtained the soap from the stores in our lorry. This came in nine inch lengths and was atrocious, unrefined, stuff. No Imperial Leather or Lux was available for Commando use. He took the soap off me and started trimming it into a long point. I was appalled at the waste as bits fell onto the floor.

I tried to voice my annoyance, but in broken English, he told me to wait. He then ushered me into the stables where a dejected donkey was tethered. The pathetic creature looked terrible, with his head gazing dispiritedly at the floor.

What the farmer did next really surprised me. He lifted up the donkey's tail and shoved the soap column up his backside. I was totally speechless with shock.

An hour later the farmer came running up to me, shouting. The constipated donkey had now relieved himself and was no longer 'poo bound'. The soap laxative had proved most effective. The donkey was vital to the running of the farm and could now resume his workload.

The farmer was extremely grateful. As a member of 41 Commando Unit, I was happy to help maintain agricultural productivity in war-torn Belgium. I had learned a most novel and drastic use for a bar of soap.

The donkey before and after its unorthodox laxative treatment. Cartoons by Jim Titley.

British Commandos aboard LCT 532 prepare to land on Walcheren island, November 1944.
"It was worse than D-Day," recalls Ted.
Photograph courtesy of the Imperial War Museum (A 26276).

After quite a few weeks' rest, the Naval Force landing craft arrived and took us to an island called Walcheren. This is a big island off the Dutch coast. It was November 1944. We were part of the 4SS, involved in Operation Infatuate 11.

It was worse than D-Day. The island was heavily fortified. The RAF had dropped super bombs onto the dykes to release the water. The area was all reclaimed land below sea level so it had flooded. We landed on the island at a place called Westkappelle which had been heavily bombed. The RAF had obliterated the town of Westkappelle but the consequence of this was the saving of thousands of Allied lives.

As we landed, a young lad came down to tell us where most of the Germans were. He was the only member of his family to have survived in the flooded cellar of a windmill where they had taken refuge during the bombing. He had left there to come and meet us.

I understand that the Dutch people knew that we were coming. Unfortunately, it does not appear that the general public were given any safety briefings. The blast from the bombs destroyed the dykes and caused the cellars to flood. Nearly all the occupants sheltering there from the bombs were drowned as a result.

After the war I met the lad in a café and asked why he honoured the RAF when they had been responsible for killing his entire family. He put his hand on my arm and answered that if it had not been for the Germans then the tragedy would not have occurred.

41 RM Commandos on Walcheren, 1944.
Image courtesy of The Commando Veterans Association,
Warwick Neild-Siddall Collection.

I admired his insight and spirit of forgiveness. I then returned to Westkappelle and laid a wreath on the grave of his family.

W E USED a tank called the 'Buffalo', which is amphibious and could travel on water or land. Buffaloes were specially designed for flooded areas and their use was an application of wonderful thinking and foresight by the organisers.

The flooding went into the gun emplacements which saved a lot of our lives but killed many Dutch people. We went from there, up around the coast. The remaining causeway for us to actually fight on, was only a mile wide as the rest of the land was under sea water. That spared a lot of the boys as all the big guns were now under water. The Germans could no longer use them.

From Westkapelle we fought on the causeway going up to Dunkirk. On our second day there, in the late evening, there was suddenly a loud bang. Two of my mates, walking in front of me, were killed by an anti-personnel mine (AP).

The mine itself was set off by pressure, such as stepping on it. It would rise about three feet out of the ground like an eerie sentinel and then explode. It contained masses of ball bearings. Unbeknown to me, one of them actually penetrated my knee. Luckily it did not smash any of the bone.

When I got hit everyone dived for shelter. That is natural instinct. We were told to dig in, using our shovels to create a hole to bury ourselves in as best we could. Luckily it was sandy ground.

The orders came to stay where we were and make ourselves as inconspicuous as possible. We were to stay there during the night as our superiors thought that there were mines ahead of us. I was unaware that a ball bearing had penetrated my knee. I simply thought that I had hurt it when I dived for the deck.

While we were lying there I shouted back to my corporal, "movements ahead corporal." He responded, "where?" I held up my hand and said, "three fingers to the right of that church tower and two fingers to the left of the windmill." The mortar team behind us were called as a result and they gave the Germans, who were laying mines, a right hammering. Sporadic firing followed.

The next morning, after we had stayed in our makeshift bunkers, we were told to get out our pig stickers (bayonets) and move forward prodding the ground in front of us to feel for mines. When we came to move forward, I was unable to move as my leg was badly swollen.

I told my number two that I could not move as my leg was so bad. He shouted to the sergeant. He answered, "right, as soon as we get a lull, get him back to the CCS (casualty clearing station)." When I was taken there, I saw that it was accommodated in a school. I told the orderly that there was something wrong with my knee. I was still ignorant of the nature of the injury.

The orderly told me that I had a hole in my trousers, which would have to be split. He observed that there was a large scab on my right knee, which would have to be cleaned off.

The invasion of Walcheren Island, November 1944. There is a Buffalo tracked vehicle in the centre of the photo. Image courtesy of the National Army Museum. Image No. 101761.

He obtained a wooden spatula with cotton wool and started to clean it up. The ball bearing was dislodged and clonked onto the ground. After he had cleaned up and dressed the wound I reported to the duty officer in that area.

I was using my rifle like a crutch for support. The duty officer refused to let me re-join my unit in this condition. He told me to get down to the landing craft on the beach and assist with the taking of prisoners to Ostend.

I went onto the ship's bridge. There were two machine gunners and myself guarding one hundred-odd German prisoners in the well deck. A rope was draped across the deck as a safeguard. Any German who crossed the line would be shot.

THE JOURNEY to Ostend was uneventful. En route the craft landed on a slipway which was in the docks at Antwerp. A Canadian regiment was in charge there and the German prisoners were handed over to them. There was a mobile canteen waiting. The German prisoners were given a mug of tea, hard tack biscuits and a cigarette if they wanted one. In those pre-public health warning days, this was considered a kindness.

After we had rested, the Canadians required the prisoners to help load the landing craft with crates. These contained ammunition and foodstuffs. The prisoners started to move but a German officer shouted something and the prisoners froze. The officer was dressed in the macabre black SS uniform. Each German regiment had an SS presence, to keep control.

The Canadian officer repeated that he wanted the prisoners to load the craft with crates. I was told this afterwards.

The German officer turned round and said that the command was against the Geneva Convention, because ammunition was being loaded. The Canadian officer retorted, "you don't know what that means, you don't know the meaning of that." The Canadian then landed a punch in the German officer's guts, causing him to crumple to his knees.

The Canadian then grabbed him by his hair and held him under the sea water, until he nearly drowned. He then dragged the German up the slipway and turned round, repeating his order to the German prisoners that they load the craft. I had never seen men move so quickly.

The Germans were Kreigsmarines, navy service men, who were older and wiser than the SS officer in charge of them. They did not want a dose of Canadian contempt meted out to them for the sake of not handling a few crates. Any scruples or principles they may have harboured over the Geneva Convention quickly evaporated.

The Canadians would have witnessed terrible cruelty during hostilities. They may have been aware of the Hitler Befehl by this stage. Consequently, they would not be sympathetic to the German officer's selective desire to follow the niceties of the Geneva Convention.

After two days, the Commandos were back on the island. When I got back I re-joined my unit. We managed to capture the whole of the island.

In Domburg, on the north west coast of Walcheren, there was a big German garrison. When the Germans capitulated the German officer thought that we comprised half the British army. When he was told that we were just a Commando unit, he turned around to our officer and saluted. He was really surprised that so a small unit could capture them.

We were sent back to one of the villages – Goes – for a rest in private billets again. I asked our landlord on Westkappelle how nasty had the Germans been. He told me that the Allies had given his people freedom from oppression. I asked him what he meant by oppression. As an example, he told me that if the Germans walked into a room, the Dutch were not allowed to lock their doors against them.

The Germans would take anything they fancied, especially food. The Germans themselves were short of food and starving. They would search gardens for vegetables. People would let the weeds grow to hide their vegetables.

Everyone kept rabbits for food. If anyone saw Germans coming they would give a special knock on the wall. This was a signal to grab the rabbits. He said, "we would put the rabbits into a cardboard box and then shake the hell out of them." By frightening them in this way, the rabbits would freeze in terror and not move for a couple of hours. The boxes were then hidden in the attic.

Gun emplacements. Cartoon by Jim Titley.

I asked our cook if he could spare a white loaf of bread. I presented it, with margarine, to the family I was billeted with. They treated it with great veneration, like Christmas cake.

It was touching to witness the reaction of the family; they had not seen white bread during the war years. People had baked tulip bulbs in the oven until they were dark brown, as a coffee substitute. That is how bad things were for them. I never told anyone about this episode, ever.

THAT entire coastline was very heavily fortified. We had strict orders not to wander around these places because of booby traps and mines. The Germans were very clever about that.

As the Germans retreated, I was always looking for something. I went around as a scrounger, reverting to my days growing up in Pembroke Dock. I used to carry a small hand torch – a pump action, just like a dynamo. I also cut a little three point branch off a tree.

I would wander down dark tunnels, contrary to orders, to get to the gun emplacements. These were big, heavy coastal guns. I used to hold the thin branch in front of me in case of trip wires. When I got down into the gun emplacement, I would look for abandoned objects. I cut the eagle and swastika badges off German uniforms as souvenirs. My mother made these into pillow cases. The Germans left empty bunk beds and bunkers when they fled.

I found a small box of fairly light cartridges. I kept these to use on the beach as targets. I could set them off. I would shoot at a cartridge and then it would explode. I tucked the box under my arm and walked back up the tunnel when I heard voices. "Oh dear, I've been caught," I thought.

I knew I was not allowed to be there. I could see light at the end of the tunnel and two figures coming down. They were just striking matches to see the way.

One said to the other, "I wonder if there are any booby traps down here?" The other one said, "the REME (Royal Mechanical and Electrical Engineers) have been here and cleared it."

Something clicked in my head. Wickedly, I dropped the box of cartridges on the floor. One grabbed the other and mischievously I hissed. One of them cried out that it was a booby trap and they scarpered back down the tunnel.

Everything in a tunnel sounds louder because of the reverberation. I ran after them to try and stop them. By the time I got to the entrance, the two men were racing down the road like a pair of Gypsy's greyhounds.

I should like to have explained my little practical joke to them. They would have been RAF personnel who were tasked with dismantling the radar station which the Commandos had captured. Looking back with hindsight, they may not have appreciated my sense of humour.

A couple of days after, I went on a clandestine visit to another bunker which stored coastal artillery shells. I got just inside the door but on this occasion I had omitted to bring my torch with me.

I could see yellow and purple discs which looked like ice cream wafers, scattered on the floor. I scooped a couple into my hand and set light to them with a match, believing them to be cardboard or paper. Little did I know that they were made of flammable cordite.

The discs ignited immediately and exploded in my hand, causing me to drop them. This caused the rest, lying on the floor, to combust. I was out of that door in an instant.

I leapt over a large, wire entanglement, not caring if there were mines present there or not. I landed on the sandy beach. Behind me rose a column of flame thirty feet high. I scrambled back to the billet.

Commandos marching through Vlissingen (Flushing) in 1944. When Ted Owens saw this photograph for the first time in January 2019, as this book was being prepared for publication, he immediately recognised himself as the soldier looking into the camera on the left of the picture! "Due to my injuries I was excused carrying a pack supported by webbing, and you can see that I'm the only Commando in the photo who does not have webbing across his body," said Ted.
Photo courtesy of the National Army Museum.

Ted's tunnel prank. Cartoon by Jim Titley.

The next day we marched past the area, on a rest period. Someone said that it was obviously a booby trap, but it had not been discovered who had set it off. I was lucky to get away with it.

EVENTUALLY, there was a big hue and cry. It was now late November 1944. We had to move out quickly to go and help the Americans at The Battle of the Bulge. The Allies termed this the Ardennes Counteroffensive.

It was nicknamed 'The Battle of the Bulge' by the press. This referred to the 'bulge' in German front lines on war time news maps. It spread to Wallonia in Eastern Belgium, north east France and Luxembourg.

During this time we travelled to S-Hertogenbosch, in Holland, colloquially known as Den Bosch. We had lifted the tin roof of a building where we were hiding, in order to keep a discreet lookout.

Two of us were on watch. Suddenly my number two nudged me in the chest. Peering out of the gap we had created between the walls and roof, two cyclists were observed approaching us. The figures began to sink behind the embankment.

I had a look through the sight of my gun. I recognized the figures as German military police. They wore silver plates across their chests denoting their identity.

I suggested a longshot but my comrade thought that it was too far to reach the target. They were about 1,100 yards away.

We waited for them to travel closer. I then told number two that I was going to risk the shot. Number two disagreed, saying that they were still too far away and that I should hang on a bit. The cyclists were now about 1,025 yards away.

I ignored this advice and took a shot at the left hand cyclist. His arms flew up in the air in an expansive gesture.

I told number two that I reckoned I had hit him. You do not ride a bicycle like that. I had put my pack on the wall as a little support and kept the gun barrel inside so that the discharge flash would be concealed.

I could not have been spotted as there was no return fire at the building which we sheltered in. We would have to watch and keep account of any reciprocal fire. Our job was to locate where the main gunfire was coming from. We reported back to the officer, telling him what we had done, what gunfire had been spotted and what movements had been observed.

About two days later our corporal informed us that a Spitfire had crashed in a field about a mile behind us. He instructed us to recover the cannons from the Spitfire which we could then utilise for extra support. As we moved towards the plane, we discovered that the Germans had flooded the land.

This meant that the plane and cannons were out of reach. Whilst we were close to the plane, we heard the whizz of a bullet passing over our heads. Automatically we dropped to one knee and scanned the area to establish where it had come from.

The only thing prominent which we could see was the church tower on the other side of the river. I logged this in my report on our return. The officer said that if there was a sniper there, that indicated an observation post. He summoned the Polish sub-tank group accompanying us. Only three rounds were fired into the tower, which was cut off completely, level with the bank. There was no further enemy gun fire.

The Germans had started to counterattack the Americans. We went to a little village which the Germans had infiltrated, especially with snipers. We were searching for them down the village street, trying to winkle them out, when a bullet passed quite close to my nose. It was as close as that. Whether it was from a sniper or a stray, I shall never know.

The bullet hit the wall alongside which I was standing. It shattered against the wall and a piece of the bullet ricocheted. It travelled right through my throat and lodged in my wind pipe. It is still there today, some seventy four years later.

The medics were very concerned about my breathing and eating. My throat was extremely sore. The doctors had to put a pipe down my throat to assist with my breathing. I was fed through a tube.

I was then moved to the Canadian hospital, where the care and kindness was exemplary. I was twenty years old and I had been injured in the November, just before peace was declared. My unit was sent to Germany but the MO declared me unfit for active service. I was to be sent back to England.

I wanted to stay, but my protests were in vain.

Back to Blighty

I WAS sent to a holding battalion which was Plymouth Division. Those who were sent there with me were also from independent units. We were not going to take orders from anyone else. We had seen live action in the raw and been injured as a result.

When we arrived at the barracks the RSM (regimental sergeant major), shouted that we should 'double', which meant run on the parade ground. We stuck our fingers up at him. He became blue with anger and spat out that we were rabble. He had never seen live action and had no conception of what we had undergone, on the battlefield of northern Europe.

Within twenty four hours, we were out of there. We were sent to Wrexham. After all that we had been through, we were put under canvas outside the camp so as not to fraternise with the other soldiers. We were considered troublemakers who would not obey orders.

It was reckoned that we would be a bad influence on anyone with whom we had contact. We were all ex-wounded or ex-prisoners of war. There was no counselling, psychotherapy or other forms of treatment. No one acknowledged what we had endured. We were simply left alone and not bothered with much.

Our psychological state was not addressed. Having made sacrifices we were now reckoned to be a confounded nuisance. The only medical concession offered was not to have to go on parade at 9am. We could just lie around. Our diet consisted of basic cookhouse meals.

An initiative test was then devised for the troublemakers. By way of getting us fit again, we were ordered to get out onto the road and up to a rendezvous in Aberdeen. We would be met there by representatives of 41 Commando. Each of us received provisions for our journey consisting of a raw potato, four slices of bread with margarine and jam.

Wartime Aberdeen, with people inspecting the aftermath of a bombing raid on the city.

Perhaps this was regarded as a psychological and physical exercise as we were not permitted to catch the train. A cynic might say that this was to save on cost. The choice was walking or hitching.

My mate and I were very lucky. He was a Birmingham boy with town ways and we got out onto the road. We hadn't got a couple of miles before we put our thumbs up to hitch a lift and an Armstrong Siddeley car stopped.

It was driven by a sales rep, but I do not know what he sold. We said that we were embarking on a journey to Scotland, but he was only going as far as Manchester. We felt that this would be a great help in any event as we should be travelling on the main road.

The salesman took us to a big hotel and bought us a meal. It was the kindness of strangers. The manager let us sleep on a sofa free of charge after the salesman recounted our story to him.

Several cars later we arrived at the Firth of Forth and the Forth Bridge. A fish lorry picked us up here. We reached Aberdeen's Victoria Monument. The army personnel at Wrexham had told us to rendezvous there, as a clue to our ultimate destination.

A sergeant and officer from 41 Commando were stationed in the cinema alongside the monument. This was to serve as the reception area for the weary travellers. Some took days to reach the end point. Others stole cars and bicycles to complete the journey.

As far as I am aware, no one was prosecuted for theft. Some just gave up and handed themselves in at local police stations. They were then collected by operatives of 41 Commando and taken to Aberdeen. It was all very cloak and dagger. Perhaps it was hoped that we troublemakers would get lost on the way.

One tragic case involved one of our number who was an extremely handsome man. A piece of metal had lodged in his skull on the side of his head. This brain damage rendered him incapable of cognition sufficient to enable him to reach Aberdeen. After two weeks he was taken to hospital. I never saw him again.

No one deserted as there was nowhere else to go and we all wanted to be demobbed. We were all allocated local billets and set forth. My friend and I were billeted with a widow. The people of Aberdeen took us in. I shall never forget the warmth, generosity and hospitality shown to the walking wounded by the Scots.

We did not have to report to the officer in charge of this operation until 9am but if the weather was bad we could remain in our billets. All we did was go down to the beach or local playing field with the only piece of equipment given to us, which was a medicine ball. We could then return to our billets at 3.30pm. No transport was laid on. We had to walk every bit of the journey.

The people of Aberdeen were absolutely wonderful. I was hardly ever sober because when we walked down the street in uniform, people would invite us into their homes for a wee dram.

If anyone says the Scots are mean, then they ought to see me, because I know differently.

I decided to try out ice skating at the local rink. There was a lack of such facilities in Pembroke Dock. I had never ventured onto a rink before.

Needless to say, I slid straight onto my back. I lay there, dazed and inert. I caught my breath and then gazed up into a fine, feminine face. This belonged to a charming young lady, who helped me up. She was about nineteen years of age with fair skin, a handsome smiling face with pale blue eyes; five feet eleven inches in height and slim. Her jet black hair was pinned in a bun, which I thought looked very elegant. Her skirt was tartan and she wore a uniform jack-

Happy landing... Ted meets an angel on the Aberdeen ice. Cartoon by Jim Titley.

et. I found her Scottish lilt delightful. I will call her Flora.

This angel of mercy then proceeded to try and teach me to skate, a skill in which she was proficient. It was a thankless task. I might have passed the Commando training but this did not include proficiency in ice skating.

I skidded and tumbled despite Flora's best endeavours to keep me upright. For the first time since being wounded for a third time, I was having fun. At the end of the session I saw Flora home. We arrived at a large, fortified house. I assumed that she was a maid or housekeeper.

She then spoke into an intercom and the gates were opened. We had a kiss and a cuddle. Then she said that she would like to see me again.

We arranged to meet the following day at the Victoria Monument. The next day saw drizzly rain and I sought shelter in the doorway of the cinema.

A large car which could have been a Morris 10, pulled up, the window was wound down and I heard a female voice call out, "Ted". My date had arrived in some style to collect me.

Soldiers on their way to be demobilised at the end of the war.
Photo courtesy of the Imperial War Museum (BU 8053)

Few people had cars or petrol in those days, so this was completely unanticipated.

I asked who the car belonged to and Flora informed me that it was hers. I was then driven towards Dundee. We met for three consecutive days. Flora always paid for everything and told me to pick up the change.

We drove around Aberdeen and visited the massive granite quarry. We also motored along the coast road and parked at the headland. We embraced and kissed. It was wonderful to hold a winsome woman in my arms after all the harsh actualities of war.

After three nights Flora suggested that I spend my remaining time in Aberdeen at her home. I advised my landlady that even though I would be moving out, she would continue to be paid for me. My mate, Ray Smith from Birmingham would remain with her in any event.

We arrived at the magnificent house and I entered the hall. It was filled with armour and the walls were covered in shields. Flora then told me that she was the lady of the house and had sent all the servants away for the night. Flora was a member of the Scottish aristocracy.

I ended up in bed with her. We became very close. She was a warm and expressive person. I had every respect for her and she for me. Flora was married and her husband was on active service. The war years were permissive times. No one knew if they would live, die or see spouses return. We cannot be judged for seizing the moment to share love, comfort and compassion.

When it came time to leave, Flora offered me her car so I could return. Flora also attempted to give me £100, which was an enormous sum in those days.

I could not take it. Flora had done so much for me but there was no future for us together. I had thought long and hard about this.

I was sorry that she was married. I believe that her husband was somewhat older than her. He was away fighting. I genuinely wished all would turn out well for her. We had both benefitted from the warmth, friendship and companionship my time in Aberdeen permitted.

Attractive, female company was a tonic in itself. I had relished the drives around the Scottish countryside, which were a rare thing just after the war. I refused her kind offers and never went back. I had appreciated my time with Flora but now I had to leave.

I SET OFF back to Wrexham with Ray to be demobbed. On approaching demob, I attempted to stay on but was deemed medically unfit.

Our journey back involved Ray getting 'piddled' and burning a bed at a YMCA. I presume that he fell asleep smoking a cigarette. We were ungraciously ejected from this accommodation. Eventually we reached Wrexham and then Plymouth where we were discharged.

I received a bespoke, blue, pin-stripe demob suit with brown shoes. My life was to continue in my home town of Pembroke Dock.

Civvy Street

ON MY return to Pembroke Dock I re-joined the fire brigade but after two years I became disenchanted. I then went to work for Marine and Port Services. Its work was mainly connected with oil tankers.

For a pastime I loved fishing and shooting. This was of great assistance to me as I used to drink a lot. I later discovered that I could have been suffering from post-traumatic stress syndrome. I had been very young when I went to war. No one offered help and advice to heal the returning combatants.

Most people of my generation never talked about their wartime experiences. We had to discover our own ways of coping. This usually meant shutting out our appalling experiences.

The Lost Boots

I used to do a lot of walking around for shooting, but only for the table, not for sport. It is terrible to think of the enormous waste of good food connected with some commercial shoots today.

I was walking along the foreshore at Cosheston Pill one day when I heard a gun going off, bang, bang, bang, with four minutes between each shot. When I came around the bend in the river, I saw a chap nearly up to his waist in the mud. He was shouting for help.

Although he could see me, he was still firing his gun to draw attention to himself. My natural instincts came to the fore. I told him to take control of himself, calm down and not struggle. I shouted to him, "take your big coat off".

I told him to lay it in front of him, opened up. I then told him to lay his gun across the front of the coat and lay his arms on the gun. This formed a pocket of air. I told him to keep still and that I would be out with him as soon as I possibly could.

Post-war Pembroke Dock. Right: Ted as he looked on his return to his home town after the war.

I then cut a mass of hazel branches and laid them on the mud, one in front of the other, which I walked across. They gave me terrific support. I did this about ten to twelve times. I laid branches on either side of him to provide sufficient weight bearing for his feet. I asked him what type of boots he was wearing.

He replied that he was wearing thigh boots. "Oh dear," I said. I then asked him to straighten his legs and point his toes straight down like a ballet dancer.

I then put my arms underneath his arms and pulled him straight out of his boots. I walked him back, bare footed now, to the beach. I returned to the spot where he had been trapped and retrieved his coat and gun. Unfortunately I was unable to ease is boots out of the constraining mud.

Being that he was now bare footed and some miles from home, I pondered on what I should do. I asked if he wanted his coat. He did not as it was now plastered with mud. I cut the arms off his coat with my knife and fashioned some impromptu footwear! To see him walk home was the funniest thing I had ever seen. His feet were like a seal's flippers, flip flopping along.

He was a local man living at Waterloo and I saw him safely home. I never mentioned the incident to my mother when I returned home that day.

The next day, the gentleman called at the door. Ozzie Lawrence was his name. My mother answered the door and Ozzie asked for me. He wanted to give me his gun as he said that he was too frightened to go out shooting again.

I told him that I had a gun and he did have two sons who might like his gun in the future.

Mother asked why I had said nothing about this rescue. I told her that I had simply taken it in my stride. I was about twenty five years old.

Cartoon by Jim Titley.

The Phantom Pheasant

There was a big old building opposite where I lived, which was used as a store and saleroom where people could sell things at auction. The person who owned the place had retired. All the remaining items were to be sold.

I worked with a group of men given the task of clearing out the property. We used the horse and cart which still belonged to the firm. Everything had to be removed from the premises. Unsold items were to be smashed into small pieces and conveyed to the tip.

Now, looking back on it, this was a terrible waste. Furniture and household items were in short supply at that time and some of the items may have been quite valuable.

Ted's wife Laurie.

Amongst the unwanted objects was a large, glass case full of stuffed pheasants. I asked the boss if I could take one of them. "By all means," he said, "help yourself."

I had it for about a week and the next time that I went out shooting I took the stuffed pheasant with me. I stuck it up in a hedge, located in a tranquil spot near the seashore. I adjusted it to look as if it was feasting on the blackberries protruding from the hedge.

I did not return that way again for a week or so. I had completely forgotten about my amusing jest. As I walked behind Bangeston Hall towards the shore, I espied a rotund pheasant enjoying a meal of blackberries in a hedge.

Quick as a flash, I took aim but in the moment that I pulled the trigger it dawned on me that I was shooting my own bird. The hoax was on me. I jumped over the hedge and kicked the poor thing flying. I was so annoyed with myself for being so stupid.

My unfortunate gundog was running around like a lunatic trying to recover what I had shot. Of course there is no smell from a stuffed bird; a gundog would use scent to locate the quarry. My prank punctured my pride in a flurry of feathers and sawdust. My good friend John would ask me to recount the tale whenever we were in company. He never tired of the joke being on me.

My Wife Laurie

I settled down and married a local girl, Laurie. Laurie had gorgeous auburn hair and had served in the forces. She served with the RAF at Hoy in Scotland during the war, dealing with aircraft movements logged with 3D models, moved with rakes on maps.

I went to live with her and her family at 29, Water Street. After about six months I palled up with a neighbour living opposite me. I knew him as John Goriah. I could not pronounce his real name.

He was nicknamed 'John' in the RAF where he had served with distinction. He and his brother Harry were volunteers from the tropical island of Mauritius. They came to this country to help us out during WWII. This was an extremely brave thing to do.

He and his brother were based at the Sea Plane Base, in Pembroke Dock. This was part of Coastal Command.

A very strong friendship was cemented between us. Both of us had seen active service but neither of us ever mentioned our experiences. When his family came along, the children visited us regularly. There were three girls and a boy. Laurie thought the world of them as if they were her own.

A Large Tiddler and Other Sporting Tales

John and I would go shooting in Cardigan and Llechryd with his brother who was friendly with the farmers up there. We would also do a lot of salmon fishing.

John bought a little twenty five foot cabin cruiser. We used to go fishing, taking the family out on the river. We caught all types of fish including rays and blue shark.

John had two friends, Jimmy and Frank Lubbock, who would visit from London. They had a smaller boat. The four of us went fishing outside 'The Heads' near to St Ann's Head.

Ted (second right) and Laurie with John's family at Freshwater West in about 1966.

We were catching mackerel – some for food and some for bait. Every time one of them reeled in a fish I would detach it from the line.

Suddenly John shouted, "oh, I've got something big here!" I was standing up and could see more than the intrepid anglers.

It was a five foot mako shark also called a blue pointer, gorging on the bait. The line snapped off with the weight of this Pembrokeshire 'Jaws'.

I told Frank to reel in his line quickly as the shark would be after his mackerel. Frank hurriedly did as he was bidden.

As he did so, he looked over the side and asked where the shark was. With precision timing the shark revealed his location, lured by the mackerel bait, rearing out of the water, his huge jagged teeth displayed in a gruesome smile about one foot from Frank's face.

I know that these fish are dangerous. They have the capacity to attack if disturbed. Poor Frank was unnerved by this unexpected encounter. He lost all angling confidence and never ventured out fishing with me again.

The Pembrokeshire 'Jaws'. Cartoon by Jim Titley.

I USED to go up river shooting ducks in the moonlight. We fished and shot at Kilpaison. Sometimes the whole family would go cockling at Kilpaison. Rakes were used to scrape away the surface sand revealing rich bounty. The cockles were gathered up and placed in a bucket, to be fattened on oatmeal at home before being cooked.

We also caught razor fish. These bivalves are also known as razor clams. I would point out the small, keyhole shaped air holes in the mud. This was evidence of the razor fish below.

The children, armed with canisters of Saxa table salt which flowed freely (for those who remember the strap line!) would pour a small heap into the hole. This would entice the razor fish to push up a false head. This was to be ignored and would fall to one side.

The razor fish then believing the coast to be clear would project itself out of the mud three or four inches searching for a briny treat. This was the cue for the children to grab it firmly and wrest it from the mud. The razor fish were then placed in a bucket and subsequently cooked for bait.

We went shooting all over the county. One night, accompanied by John and some friends, I went fishing at St Govans, on the military range. We were oblivious to the warning notices, stating that the army were firing that night.

We had only been there an hour and a half when a Tannoy message was broadcast to us from the cliffs. We were ordered to get our arses up to the top of the cliff. Apparently we were hindering the Germany army's nocturnal manoeuvres at a cost of thousands of pounds!

When we returned to the main road I told my companions that we were in real trouble. They were very subdued at what awaited us. John was mortified at the prospect of a criminal record. The commanding officer gave us a severe telling off in the guard house and took down our details.

The military police then frogmarched us back to the car parked on the top of the cliff. We dreaded the reaction of the German soldiers we had delayed, as we passed on our way. It was our good fortune that the Germans soldiers saluted our arrival. It appeared to them that we were officers travelling with the benefit of a military police escort!

John's boat 'Molly' beached at East Llanion.

Two of the men, a father and son, with us on the night of the postponed military manoeuvres, subsequently lost their lives at St Govans near to Fisherman's Rock. They had ventured down there during a storm with a friend who suffered from cerebral palsy. At that time he was referred to as being spastic. That term is no longer used.

What induced them to visit the area in such conditions, I will never know. It is possible that they were trying to determine the path furthest out to sea, taken by cod on their journey to Sully Island at Cardiff. Numerous cod used to swim around the beaches of Cardiff in the 1960s.

The three of them were swept out to sea from Fisherman's Rock. The friend was washed back in by the tide. Scratched, bleeding and soaking wet, he managed to clamber up to the footpath. Two late night walkers encountered him and called for an ambulance and the police.

Sgt James of Pembroke Dock police force knocked on my door. I lived close to the police station and the sergeant knew that I was an experienced fisherman. He asked if I knew where Fisherman's Rock was as two men had been swept out to sea from there. I told him that I knew the location well.

The sergeant asked for my assistance in tracing them. I readily agreed and accompanied him and two constables in a car to St Govans. A high tide and ferocious wind greeted our arrival. I advised the sergeant to call off the search until the following morning as it was too dangerous to search under those treacherous conditions.

At first light the police picked me up again. The coast guards awaited us and requested that we line up and walk along an area of the cliff top which was about a mile wide. I questioned the reason for that. My local knowledge of the tides led me to suggest that there were only two areas where the men might be found. The men might be discovered at either Bull Slaughter Bay or Flimston Bay. I walked straight over to Flimston Bay. Here I saw a body on the beach. I called the police back as they were heading for Bull Slaughter Bay.

The police were not willing to chance climbing down the vertiginous cliff to reach the body. I knew the way so climbed down alone. I reached the body and turned it over.

I had found the son who had drowned, still wearing his waterproofs. He did not appear to have tried to remove any of his clothing to free his body and swim to safety.

By this time a helicopter had arrived. One of the crew was lowered down and the body was winched up. The crewman announced that the helicopter would return for me. I declined the kind offer and climbed back up the cliff.

On reaching the top, I informed the police and coastguard that the father would either be here or at Bull Slaughter Bay which was due south east. Outside the bay was a large rock. The doomed man was spread eagled on top of it. His watch and a single sock were all he now wore.

I knew that he suffered with a bad heart. How he had managed to remove his waterproofs in such atrocious conditions will always be a mystery to me. Regrettably the tide and wind had proved too fierce and he too had drowned. People should never underestimate the power of the wind and sea.

My Goose was Cooked

I went up river shooting with a mate. We rowed from Front Street intent on a late evening shoot for wild ducks.

It was extremely cold. We got as far as Benton Woods. There were huge rafts of duck. They would fly from the water for about 100 yards and then settle again. We kept the same pace of rowing five or six times, each time getting closer.

Suddenly my mate said, "don't shoot, look in front." I obeyed him and saw six Canada geese before us.

We got close enough and bowled over three of them with our guns. We struggled to lug them into the boat. I commented on their terrific wing span and stretched out the wings of one of the birds.

One of the wings had been clipped meaning that it had been placed in the river by someone, probably for a reason. Imagine our discomfiture when we read the local paper the following week. Sir Peter Scott the famous ornithologist and conservationist together with R M Lockley the highly-respected Welsh ornithologist and naturalist were attempting to make the top end of the river by Llangwm a conservation area.

To this end they had introduced some Canada geese with clipped wings to attract additional birds. The geese were there to attract other geese. As birds had gone missing – and could not have flown away – the two distinguished men could only conclude that part of their bird management had ended up on someone's table. Criticism was cast at the culprits.

Ironically there are too many birds there now and the area is overpopulated with Canada geese. They can now be shot to reduce numbers. Obviously we were ahead of our time! As it was, the fowl made fine eating for two hungry and blameless men.

Through John's brother, we met a German farmer at Whitland. He permitted us to shoot on his land. We were seeking pigeons. He informed us that there were three big fields where many pigeons roosted at night.

Ted's angling skills haven't deserted him,
as he proved on a recent visit to a Llawhaden fishery.
Photo courtesy of Mark Llewellin.

He warned us that the fourth field contained a large bull, which we should be careful of. John innocently asked, "how will I recognise the bull?"

The farmer responded in broken English, "dat is quite easy – a bull has one teat and a cow has four." Poor John looked quite humiliated. We dined out on that joke for many years.

Our favourite spot for fishing was at the back of Bangeston Farm. I would take a huge number of worms with me as bait. The fish would bite like mad. They often comprised 1lb-1.5lb sea bass. I would sink a half 45 gallon metal drum into the mud.

It would flood and I would put the catch into it. I would then select the best and let the tide take the remainder away. We fishermen conserved a lot of fish that way. There was no waste and smaller fish would then have a chance to develop and breed instead of being discarded.

Barbarous Building Sites

I went to work on a building site in Bush Street. Here are some of the things which I encountered and how I responded, without even thinking. These events occurred in the early 1960s.

One of the young lads on the site did not realise that there were no brakes on the tractor. This was very much the pre-health and safety era. He jumped on it to drive away, but the tractor belted off, out of control as there were no brakes to stop it. It was a large Ferguson tractor. It ran into one of the footings which we were building and spun upside down. The whole weight of the tractor was upon the lad's chest. The unfortunate victim was David Limmige of Church Street.

I happened to encounter the scene and spot this happening. Most of the other men had gone for a break. I grabbed a scaffold pole and jammed it underneath the tractor. Another chap close to me tried to help me to lift the tractor with the scaffold pole.

At any other time this would have been an impossible feat. However my willing assistant was a big boy, a Gypsy by the name of Moses Mocken who lived at the Gypsy encampment at Waterloo. Moses was an affable person about twenty five years old.

With Herculean effort both of us managed to lift the tractor up. By this time another worker came over to us. I told him to pull David out, but the worker was afraid of hurting him. I retorted that he could not be hurt any more than he already was.

When David was pulled out, his eyes had popped out from their sockets and lay on his cheeks due to the extreme pressure. His body was black with bruising from the waist up.

He suffered massive internal bleeding. He was taken to hospital where he convalesced for a few months. I believe that fortunately he did not lose his sight.

ABOUT a month after that we had a JCB on site. The driver was moving earth across the road with the bucket. A young man was walking backwards, talking to someone and heading straight towards the bucket.

I thought that if I shouted he would turn and look at me, losing valuable seconds to get out of the way. I ran up to him as fast as I could and rugby tackled him to the ground. Unfortunately, the bucket of the JCB caught him on the side of the head causing a nasty cut.

Nevertheless he was a very lucky young man, when one considers what could have happened.

He was a mixed race lad. His father had been a black GI stationed at Llanion Barracks in Pembroke Dock who had an anvil tattooed on his arm. This was very much a distinguishing feature of that GI.

The lad's mother was a local lady, Miss Jones. He was brought up by the Armitage family in Pembroke Dock. His father had been killed during the war, never knowing that he had a son.

Perils at Pendine

I saved the lives of three men in the early sixties at Pendine Sands, of Donald Campbell and Bluebird fame. I was fishing on the beach when a van drove towards me on the sands.

I attempted to wave it down as there was a dangerous gully through which I was waiting for the tide to gush. The driver passed me and continued over the sands. I knew that the driver had driven his passengers into the gully.

I could barely see the top of the van in the distance. After about ten minutes one of the passengers in the van, came running back towards me. He pleaded for me to fetch a tow rope to get the van back to safety. I advised him that there was no time for that as they were some four miles from the road.

I told him to sprint back to his mates and race back with them as fast as they could, as the tide would be surging through the chasm at any time. I stressed in no uncertain terms that the men should get back to me as soon as possible or there would be trouble.

By the time the men hastened back, the tide was already flowing through the gully, well over their knees. They were extremely fortunate. They said they would return the next day to salvage the van which was full of electrical equipment.

The van had been driven from Pembroke Dock without the owner's knowledge or permission. The van ended up at Laugharne, five miles away, as a hunk of metal, bashed by the tide which flowed faster than one could walk.

I asked the men if they had heard my whistle which I always carried for safety reasons. One turned around and answered, "yes, but we thought that you had received it as a Christmas present."

They presumably thought that I was trying out this juvenile gift, for fun. That was their reckless attitude. It was a January day with few people about. They were extremely fortunate that I was present.

THE following year Taffy, my friend, and I went fishing at the far eastern side of Pendine, Ginst Point. As I arrived I could see that over the gully there were two men and a boy. I shouted at them to return as the tide was already coming through. It swirled forwards, already knee deep.

Such was the power of the sea that it was difficult to walk through by the time that I had reached them. I told them to cast their fishing lines across to me. I intended to twist the lines across my arm to give them support to wade through the turbulent water.

The young lad was rigid with terror and would not do as I asked. He was accompanied by his father and another gentleman. The adults could not leave the boy stranded, so they all retreated half a mile down the beach to a sandbank.

I asked Taffy to run back to his car and drive to the nearby Pendine military camp and seek help at the police guard room. The message was duly received and a signal was sent out for the inshore lifeboat to be launched. I think that Tenby would have been the closest to us. When Taffy returned he told me that the inshore lifeboat was on its way.

In the meantime, an air sea rescue helicopter was coincidently flying back to Chivenor in Devon and had picked up the signal. No 22 Squadron RAF had operated a Search and Rescue Flight since 1956. It was disbanded in 2014. They flew Westland Whirlwind, Westland Wessex and Westland Sea King helicopters.

The helicopter, which I believe was a Sea King, was only a couple of miles away and flew to the crisis scene. It hovered over the men and boy. By this time the water was up to their waists. They were using their fishing rods as stabilisers to hold them against the tide. They must have been absolutely terrified.

One of the crew members was lowered down on a winch wire. There was not time to winch them all up individually, so he picked them up all in one go. This was not normal procedure during an air sea rescue.

The hapless victims were not winched into the helicopter. All three were simply winched above the water and flown to

A RAF Sea King similar to that involved iu the rescue at Pendine.

the beach. They were gently deposited on the sand, where they collapsed in a petrified heap. They were mute with shock, the horrifying ordeal and unorthodox rescue having robbed them of the power of speech.

I approached the winchman and shook his hand, thanking him for his skill and bravery. I gave a thumbs up to the pilot saying 'well done'.

The winchman asked for the names and addresses of the bedraggled group and then the rescuers were gone. It was a wonderful feat of rescue. Fortune had smiled on this doomed fishing trip.

Breaking My Silence

I COME from a generation which did not articulate the pain or the horror of the war years. Like so many others, I had internalised my war time experiences. Alcohol or tears were my only solace, to be borne in private.

How I first broke my silence came about in an extraordinary way some 64 years later. I had trouble with damp in my council house. A councillor visited my home late one evening to inspect the problem for himself. I had two mates visiting at the time. They sat on the settee, intent on planning a fishing expedition.

Meanwhile, the councillor entered the house to conduct his examination. He then announced that the damp emanated from the kitchen. I remonstrated that the council had unwisely filled in the space between the cavity walls. This was causing the whole house to sweat. Therein lay the problem.

He disagreed, saying, "no, no, no it is not that". The councillor then returned to my bedroom and pointed to a glass of water alongside my bed. Here, he concluded, was the cause of the damp and condensation.

I nearly hit the roof at this preposterous conclusion. I was incensed at his attitude. He must have thought that I was a senile old fool to make such a remark.

I roared, "you come up here and talk to me like that. What have you done in your life apart from push a pen?"

I really went to town on him and used every swear word in the book. I told him that as a teenager, I had been knocked unconscious by a mine in Pembroke Dock. I was wounded abroad three times on active WWII service and he had the damn cheek to patronise me in my own home. It was a feeble attempt on his part to evade responsibility.

He must have presumed that I was gullible enough to swallow his absurd judgement. He had another think coming. He left with his tail between his legs.

I then walked in on my two friends who were waiting in my sitting room. One, Colin Belmain, said that in the twenty years he had known me, he never knew that I had such a ferocious temper. I had never talked about my war record so he said that he was completely unaware of it.

The other friend Harry Jones, was a school teacher. He was a very agreeable, mild man who was small and quiet. After this enlightening episode, every time we went out together, he kept quizzing me about my war time encounters.

Initially I got annoyed with him. Having sublimated these memories for so long, it was very difficult to express them coherently. Eventually I began to break my silence and answer some of his questions.

We happened to go to the Pater Hall to listen to a talk given on Coastal Command. This was a topic which I had great interest in. Unfortunately the speaker failed to arrive. An announcement was made that he had been taken ill.

This was a great disappointment. Rather than cancel the evening, a request was made for anyone present to share any suitable story with the restless audience. Colin leapt up, proclaiming that what Ted had told him would open people's eyes. I had participated in a very important part of history and was still alive to tell the tale.

I shook my clenched fist at him and urged him to sit down. I had no great ambitions as an orator. Initially I lacked confidence to voice memories which had been subsumed for almost seventy years. Colin was insistent that I address the audience and share my story with them. I could feel myself trembling. I had never spoken in public before.

Ted at Wings Over Carew in 2016 with the airfield's restored WWII control tower in the background.
Photograph: John Evans

Ted returns to Achnacarry.

The audience consisted of about fifty local people who began encouraging me to tell my tale. I struggled to my feet as I am not so nimble these days. Strangely, once I began to speak, I stopped shaking.

My thoughts and voice flowed and I produced a smooth delivery. It was a story that needed to be told and I progressed as if I had been a public speaker all my life. I actually shocked myself. I really got into my stride and I have not stopped telling my story since.

I HAVE given talks to many school children at all the primary and secondary schools in Pembrokeshire. The last school which I spoke at was in Wrexham.

I fully enjoy myself and I know that I am doing good to the children when they listen to my stories. These are not fairy stories but real situations which I have found myself in. The children are often intrigued by my service dagger. I warn them that this was an instrument of war and that knives are not toys.

If they see anyone brandishing a bladed weapon they should tell a parent or person in authority. I hope that this may prevent an avoidable tragedy. Many youngsters do not realise the actual potential for harm which a bladed weapon carries. I emphasise that it is not glamourous or cool to carry one.

As a result of going public on my war experiences I have been invited to the Commando units at Plymouth, Portsmouth, and Chivenor. These Commando units are mostly attached to the marines in some form or another.

I was invited back to Achnacarry at Fort William, where I trained. It had been seventy years since I was last there. This is all thanks to Mark Llewhellin who was in 29 Commando based in Hereford.

I have met all the SAS boys based in Hereford. Many of them have done me the honour of visiting me at home, here in Pembroke Dock. Bear Grylls and others posed for a photograph with me when I visited the SAS unit based at Poole. I also attended a ceremony of remembrance at Le Grande in France in 2016.

I attended a function at the SAS officers' mess in Plymouth where I met Bill Billingham who is a bodyguard. I walked to the table with all the officers.

When I went to sit down there was a terrific bang. I thought that someone must have fired a big gun outside. Everything shook, the tables shook and I was knocked slightly off balance, such was the intensity of the explosive force. My response to the vibration caused everyone to look at me.

The photographer and captain sitting next to me had heard nothing. Then the second staff lieutenant waved at me and said that this phenomenon had occurred before. Other visitors had experienced an explosion as I had done.

I asked what he meant. He told me that during the 1940s the mess hall was a marine dormitory. Six or seven marines were blown to smithereens by a bomb. The lieutenant explained that I was experiencing this horrendous incident. Perhaps I am a very sensitive person and pick up on these supernatural events.

Ted with John Mercer MP, Mark Llewhellin, Billy Billingham and Bear Grylls. Photograph courtesy of Mark Llewhellin

Revelling in Royalty

My life has become rich and full as the result of my wartime experiences. Greg Lewis, a family friend, took me to Omaha Beach on 4th June 2004 for a commemorative service attended by Her Majesty the Queen.

A large number of ex-service men had attended. We stood silent and dignified in the large cemetery as the Queen passed. One man standing near me became overwhelmed by the occasion and started praising the Queen, commenting on her appearance in the flesh. He called out, "Ma'am, you look so beautiful. I did not know that you were so beautiful."

Her Majesty, in her chic mauve coat and hat, swept past her voluble admirer and stopped to have a few words with me. "Did you fight in this area?" she asked. "No Ma'am," I said, "I fought on Sword Beach at the other end of the country. I got very badly injured on a beach at Walcheren and at the Battle of the Bulge."

Her Majesty replied, "oh, you went over the top once too often."

Royal Marines family day at Lympstone. Back row, left to right: David (Dai) O'Toole; Deputy Commander General Brigadier Hadyn White ADC; Mark Llewhellin; Major General Charlie Strickland OBE. Front: Léon Llewhellin (Mark's son) and Ted Owens.

I responded, "yes Ma'am, I don't think they liked my face!"

Her Majesty burst out laughing. Her Majesty continued her walk, deaf to the idolatry of her fan.

One of the senior officers then approached me. He was curious to know what I had said to make our monarch laugh. I repeated my humorous quip. "Well done," he replied.

At Omaha Beach I also met a Japanese representative in full regalia together with Belgian, Dutch and Canadians. The most gratifying part was when the French police brought their rifles up into the salute.

Ted (right) and other veterans chat with the Duchess of Cambridge.

Guests were seated in four tiers next to a monument. Sitting on the grass alongside were French police dog handlers with German shepherd dogs (Alsatians). Walking along the top step was a cat, which spotted the dogs.

One could tell by the cat's slow and deliberate movements that it hoped to move away unnoticed by its canine foes. Roguishly, I barked like a dog – much to the terror of the cat, which then fled.

The Japanese dignitary was in tears, laughing at my comedy turn. Luckily the police had spotted the cat, but the dogs had not. My human bark must have been pretty good to convince the French feline to flee.

I have met the Duchess of Cambridge at Aramauche Beach where a special tent was erected for a celebration meal. The Duchess chatted to a number of ex-servicemen on her table. One was a coxswain of landing craft and another was a marine. I told her about being wounded in France on D-Day, on Walcheren Island and during the Battle of the Bulge. She sympathised, remarking that I had must have had a rough time.

Princess Anne rode in a horse and trap in Cardiff when I was present. The Princess Royal spoke to me, asking if I was an ex-soldier. I confirmed that I was before she continued on her way.

Ted with an Australian army captain at an event in Milford Haven to mark the 70th anniversary of the D-Day landings.

When Prince Philip visited Pembroke Castle I was one of five ex-servicemen standing outside flanking the route which he would take to enter. Prince Philip approached me and said, "Royal Marine?" I acknowledged that he was my commanding officer. He agreed, as he was then Captain General of the Royal Marines, a role now filled by Prince Harry. He asked if I had seen active service and I told him that I had. "Well done," he said.

I have been awarded the Diplome by the Republique Francais, Ministere de la Defense, Secretariat D'Etat a'la Defense, Charge des Anciens Combattants, Counseil Regional De Basse-Normandie.

I hold the French Chavalier in the Orde National de la Legion d'Honneur.

I also have a certificate presented by the Ambassador of the Kingdom of the Netherlands, as a token of gratitude for contributing to the liberation of the Netherlands during World War II.

I have the Commando Entrainment Medal, 40 Commando Marines Medal, Termoli Port Said, Al Faw and a medal from 29 Commando Regiment Royal Artillery.

Additionally I have been decorated with the 39-45 War France & Germany medal, the Defence medal, The Victory Medal, Wound Medal, Normandy D-Day Veterans medal and the D Troop No. 41 – Royal Marine Commando medal.

In November 2018 it was my privilege to be invited to a commemmoration service in Westkappelle. I was presented with a medal from the Dutch Commandos who consider the Commandos of Achnacarry to be the fathers of their unit.

Mr George Edward Owens

Chevalier in the Ordre national de la Legion d'honneur

B Troop,
No 41
Royal Marine Commando

Some of Ted's many awards and diplomas paying tribute to his wartime service.
Photos courtesy of Pete Bounds Photography.

Ted is tempted to relive the motorcycling days of his youth. Photograph by Martin Cavaney.

Facing the Future

On 11th August 2017, I attended the annual wreath-laying ceremony at Freshwater West to commemorate the seventy five marines and six sailors who drowned off the coast there during the war.

My legs had given out so I could not lay a wreath as I had done in previous years. I sat by my car, as I still drive.

One of the officers approached me and asked why I was not participating. I explained that my legs were no longer able to support me walking up the sand bank to lay a wreath. He asked if I was active now and I replied that I was not.

He told me to hang on and he would fetch someone to talk to me. Someone duly arrived and asked how long I had been inactive. I explained that it had been for about twelve months. I had suffered difficulty with wreath-laying in 2017.

The gentleman then asked if I had received assistance from the British Legion. He was furious to learn that I had been a member since 1944, but had never received any help or assistance. However, I did admit to not actually seeking help as I did not like begging.

I'm afraid that I incurred his displeasure when I said this to him. He assured me that aiding veterans was the purpose

A mannequin wearing a gas mask brings back memories at Pembroke Dock Heritage Centre. Photograph by Martin Cavaney.

of organisations such as the one which he represented. It was certainly not begging. He was from the SSAFA (formerly The Soldiers' and Sailors' Families Association). He requested my name, rank, regiment number and who I had served with. This took place on 11.11.17.

On the following Monday morning, three men from SSAFA arrived at my house. They sat on my settee and started interrogating me. I was asked about my rent and duly produced my rent book for inspection.

SSAFA obviously contacted the appropriate channels after they took their leave of me. Within four days I received a cheque from the council as it appears that I had overpaid. My war pension also came under scrutiny and it may come to pass that I am entitled to additional payments.

One of the other men asked how long my carpets had been laid. I advised him that the carpets were about twenty six years old. "Right," he said, "we shall put new carpet in."

Two weeks later fitters from a carpet company based in Cardiff arrived on my doorstep. They transformed my home with superlative new carpeting throughout. It was tremendous how hard they worked to make all the difference.

My only regret is that my wife Laurie did not live to appreciate the luxury of new, fitted, carpets. Laurie was extremely house proud and would have rejoiced in this update to our living conditions.

The chair I sat in whilst receiving my guests had been given to me by a friend whose father had died. The SSAFA rep concluded that it was out of date. Two days later, as a result of SSAFA's intervention, a lady arrived to measure me for a new chair.

I am now the proud owner of an ergonomically designed electric chair adapted to my specific measurements. I was next asked about the age of my twelve inch screen television. I could not remember how many years I had owned it. It was certainly old. It was replaced by a brand new, large screen model.

I do not watch much television but news and wild life programmes now spring to life with sharpness and clarity.

My double bed was the next topic for discussion. It was all right but rather low. This meant with my ambulant restrictions, it was difficult to get in and out of bed. I disliked single beds.

My old bed has been superseded by a new double bed and mattress courtesy of SSAFA. The bed is much higher and consequently easier for me to get in and out of. Oh boy, can I sleep on that. It is really comfortable.

Digging myself into a sandy hole for the night, hugging my rifle for company and being attacked by hungry rats are but distant memories.

MY LAUNDRY arrangements were the next topic for discussion. I explained that my devoted friend and proxy daughter, Debbie dealt with this. "Right," said the rep. "We shall provide a new washing machine." I thought no more about this.

About a week later I had a phone call from Currys stating that I had placed an order which they wished to deliver. I was perplexed as I had not ordered a curry.

The caller was adamant that there was an order in my name. I asked if it had been paid for and was told that it had been. I did stress that I had not placed an order but was happy to receive it as it had been paid for.

I waited in that night, pleased that someone's mistake meant that I would have a free curry delivered. I was very disappointed as nothing materialised. Four days later a SSAFA rep contacted me to ask why I had cancelled the order for the new washing machine.

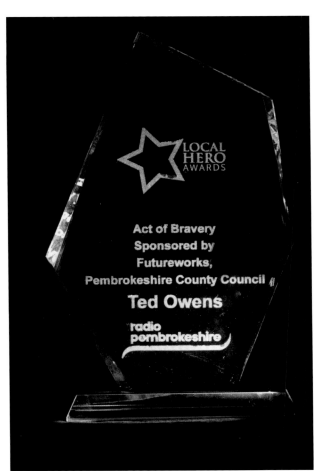

Some of Ted's awards, photographed by Pete Bounds.

Ted at home with his memories.
Photo courtesy of Pete Bounds Photography.

I protested that I had done nothing of the sort. I was told that the order had been placed with Currys but when Currys contacted me, I had denied any knowledge of it.

The penny finally dropped! I presume that Currys did not want to deliver an item where confusion reigned over its ownership. What a senior moment. Still I had a good laugh and I am the proud owner of a modern, efficient, washing machine.

Again, my dear Laurie would have been delighted with the transformation it makes to daily life. I am very grateful for that chance meeting at Freshwater West. I am very proud of SSAFA. Their support has made this ninety four year old veteran feel valued.

In the Present

In May 2018 I went to our local maritime museum in Pembroke Dock. In the corner I spotted a small boat which was called a dinghy. I asked how the dinghy had been acquired.

I was told that it had been donated by a lady from Neyland. It had belonged to her late husband. I recognised it as a boat I had owned in the 1950s.

The manager told me that this was impossible. I retorted that it was not impossible and I would tell him why this was. A Sunderland crew, flying back from Holland, in the early 1950s, spotted this dinghy in the English Channel. It was thought that there might be someone on board, so the plane was landed. It was such a beautiful little boat but it bobbed on the water empty.

The RAF crew pulled it in through the bomb bay as it was a pity to leave it in the sea. It then languished in the hangar in Pembroke Dock for a couple of years. The RAF boys used it for recreation.

Ted Owens' original Commando dagger (left), together with a more recent replica.

Ted with his old dinghy in the local Maritime Museum.

When they started dismantling the RAF station in Pembroke Dock, Wing Commander Mortley who I used to go shooting with, asked if I would like the dinghy. I collected it from the hangar laid across my pushbike.

I then rowed it on the River Cleddau from Front Street in Pembroke Dock, to Lawrenny. I was very popular on the river. Everyone recognised me, as I managed to get hold of a little outboard motor and could travel up and down the Cleddau River. I never sat down in the dinghy. I would lean to the left or right, whichever way I wanted to go, so I was easily identified.

But, after four years I became fed up having to go looking for it. Children were able to handle the dinghy as it was small. After using it, the children did not bother to tie it up. I had to cycle up and down the river searching for it.

I was worn out with this quest and sold it to a man in Milford Haven. I called the dinghy *My Girl* but her new owner called her *Bob*. It can still be seen at the Maritime Museum in Pembroke Dock. After all these years it turned up.

Strange things happen to 'Ted, the Welsh Goat Hero'. I hope they continue to do so for some time yet.

© Ted Owens

Further reading: *Flying Boat Haven* by John Evans (ISBN 1870745 04 3); *Straddle: Webfoot War Dog* by John Evans (ISBN 1870745 17 8); and *Pembrokeshire Under Fire* by Bill Richards.